Steam Memories: 1950's – 1960's

No. 13: Northumberland & North

Including: *52A, 52B, 52C, 52D, 52E, 52F, 52G, 52H, 52J & 52K*

Copyright Book Law Publications 2009
ISBN 978-1-907094-44-6

INTRODUCTION

My first memories of railways go back to pre-1950 when, as a very small child, my older brother, as with many other children in those post-war days, went train watching. I can still hear my mother saying "If you're going to watch the trains, take the 'bairn' or you're not going", so I was thrown into a pushchair and wheeled down to Heaton Junction to watch the big blue engines.

In the summer of 1955 my cousin from London came to stay, and being a spotter, wanted to visit the engine sheds around Newcastle, so it was my job to find out where they were and how to gain entry. The big lads at school knew all the angles, so drawn maps and instructions were provided on how to get there and all the illegal entries. So my foray into sheds at Gateshead, Blaydon, Borough Gardens and Tyne Dock had began, Heaton was excluded, as there was the added danger of crossing the electrified third-rail.

In the Fifties, Newcastle area engine sheds were categorised with the code 52 so the main shed, Gateshead on the south side of the Tyne, became 52A, this was the main passenger shed in the north-east, having a stud of Gresley and Peppercorn Pacifics consisting A4s, A3s, A1s and A2s. For mixed traffic turns V2s, B1s, V1/3 and G5s were utilised and J39s for trip working. Y1/3s shunted coal wagons on Dunston staithes, while J71s and J72s were used on station pilot duties at Newcastle (Central) and for shunting in yards at the west end of Gateshead. Of the six N10s allocated to work the Tanfield branch, two would be sub-shedded at Bowes Bridge at any one time. The area has since been cleared and 'Ochre yards', an exclusive housing estate, has been built on the site. Many of the addresses bear the names of former Gateshead Pacifics, a situation which came about as a result of a suggestion made by another local photographer Trevor Ermel.

Many thanks to photographers and friends Ian Falcus, Howard Forster, Chris Campbell, Ian Spencer, Peter Robinson, Barry Nicholson, George Armstrong, the late Frank Coulton, the late Eric Wilson courtesy Alan Brooks, the late Roy Stevens courtesy John Lambard, the late I.H.B.Lewis, The late Bill Longstaff courtesy Ray Kitching, A.R.Goult and Alan Thompson of the Armstrong Photographic Trust for the use of Bill Hampsons(The Bishop) and the late Jack Armstrong and Cecil Sandersons collections

A very special thank you goes to my long suffering wife Judith, for putting up with my lifelong obsession with railways and helping with the captions. My proof reading supremo Howard also gets a special thank you.

David Dunn, Cramlington, 2009.

(*Cover*) **See Page 5**

(*Title Page*) **See Page 58**

Printed and bound by The Amadeus Press, Cleckheaton, West Yorkshire
First published in the United Kingdom by Book Law Publications, 382 Carlton Hill, Nottingham, NG4 1JA

52A - GATESHEAD

After the closure of Kings Cross shed in June 1963, most of their remaining Pacific locomotives were transferred to Peterborough's New England shed for a while, prior to moving on to Scotland, Grantham, Doncaster or, much more likely, withdrawal. During their active time at New England, the A4s became very frequent visitors to Tyneside and together with most of the eight Gateshead A4s and visiting the 'streaks' from Haymarket, it became usual for as many as twelve A4s to be 'on-shed' at Gateshead at one time or another during a working day (the record was in fact sixteen A4s! but the date of that event escapes me). This particular view, taken on Saturday 22nd June 1963, focuses on the east end of the yard. This area, at the 'buffer-ends', and which was situated behind the coaling stage, was known as 'the Field' by Gateshead's enginemen. Shown, from left to right: Nos.60006 SIR RALPH WEDGWOOD, 60018 SPARROW HAWK, and 60034 LORD FARINGDON. On the left of the picture, across the running lines, can be seen the elevated stabling point at Chaytors Bank with stored steam locomotives sharing the premises with main-line diesel locomotives. The large wooden structure dominating the right side of the picture is the rear wall of the coaling stage - no mechanical aids here for servicing steam locomotives. It is a shame that the last real congregation of the A4 class took place at Gateshead, the depot's reputation for being mean with the cleaning cloths and paraffin, being doggedly adhered to during the final decade of steam traction on British Railways. Nevertheless, this wonderful reminder of what it was really like is something to be cherished by all those who witnessed BR steam first hand. As for those of you who came afterwards, relish this feast of views for what they are - a reminder of past glories, filth, grime, graft and sheer hand work, all long gone, never to return. *I.Falcus.* 3

Newcastle was the only city in the country to which all of the A4 class worked in normal service. In fact, on a summer Saturday in the late 1950s and early 1960s, it was possible to see more than twenty of the class on Tyneside. Unusually, after having been coaled, a trio of A4s have been stabled in a line at the eastern end of Greensfield engine shed, Gateshead, on Saturday 20th April 1963. Naturally, leading the field was No.60022 MALLARD, with No.60001 SIR MURROUGH WILSON coming up next and No.60025 FALCON acting as 'tail-end Charlie'. In the background, above the last two 'Streaks' is the new diesel depot fashioned from a couple of the former steam roundhouses but nevertheless an impressive depot for the new traction. Identifiable in this picture, taken from the Chaytors Bank side of the running lines, are an English Electric Type 4, a couple of 'Peaks' and, hiding behind our illustrious trio, the new ECML diesel era 'streak' the Deltic. Interesting place this, whatever your persuasions. *H.Forster.*

4

This view, taken from a position just behind the previous illustration, on 1st June 1963, illustrates the non-segregation of diesels and steam at Greensfield during busy periods. Normally, diesels were maintained in the newly created main shed and also stood outside that building. Pacifics and V2s used the long three-road straight 'Pacific' shed (built by the North Eastern Railway for the introduction of the Raven 4-6-2s in 1922) at the western end of the site. The 'smaller' steam locomotives congregated in and near the remaining roundhouse (which was de-roofed during 1964-65 and at the same time that the 'Pacific shed was demolished), also at the west end of the yard. A nice line up of ECML power, engines are: A3 No.60061 PRETTY POLLY, A4 No.60025 FALCON and 'Deltic' No.D9011 THE ROYAL NORTHUMBERLAND FUSILIERS. The three locomotives each represent a separate era from ECML history. The A3 (A1 before rebuilding) being Gresley's answer to the heavier trains coming into service at the end of the pre-Grouping period. The A4 represents the era of luxury, speed, decadence and image introduced during the post Depression years before W.W.II. The Deltic, which was the ultimate in diesel locomotion when the prototype was introduced by English Electric in 1955, became the mainstay of the ECML diesel locomotive fleet dedicated to high-speed passenger services before and after the end of steam. All three are milestones to be appreciated and respected. Luckily preserved examples of each type exist - just. *C.Campbell.*

The railway authorities did not always appreciate the need to have an uncluttered background to a portrait shot or landscape view of a locomotive. Obviously in this view, recorded in 1962, no thought was given by the shunting crew as to where to place this A2 with a clear sky behind so, in consequence of their careless attitude to the poor photographers, we have a whacking great, multi-armed, telegraph pole appearing to stick out of the top of the locomotive's tender! Never mind eh! Peppercorn single-chimney A2 No.60530 SAYAJIRAO of Haymarket shed (it certainly was not a 'local' in that condition), on 16th June 1962 'parked' on Chaytor's Bank, formerly part of the Gateshead locomotive works, but latterly used for stabling locomotives awaiting repair or storage. No.60530, as can be seen, comes into the former category. At the time, the Pacific was less than four weeks out of Doncaster works after undergoing a General overhaul and repaint. It is shown to have its leading coupled wheels removed for attention and is awaiting their return from Doncaster. The necessary wheel changes would have been carried out using the 'wheel-drop' at the rear of the 'Pacific' shed. I thought all the LNER Atlantics had been withdrawn by 1951! In the left background a newly arrived 'Peak' (this would have been D169 or D170, later to become Class 46 under the TOPS scheme and part of a large batch allocated to Gateshead depot from new) shows off its immaculate green livery before starting work in earnest. *C.Campbell.*

Another Chaytor's Bank view showing K2 No.61767, of Boston shed, and the powerful lines of an unidentified K3 awaiting attention in the repair road on 31st May 1958. The K2s were regular visitors to Gateshead because the Eastern Region members of the class had to travel to Cowlairs works in Glasgow for General overhauls and other repairs. No.61767 was in fact only a couple of weeks out of works, and must have required a minor repair on its way home to Lincolnshire. The splendid North Eastern Railway signal and its two 'dollies' separating the engines, was now in its final year of service. *C.Campbell.*

A splendid view of G5 No.67281, of South Blyth shed, at Chaytor's Bank on 10th July 1957. The 0-4-4T was just out of Gateshead works after its final General overhaul. The engine appears to have been just 'lit up' judging by the black smoke coming out of the cab. Note the push and pull gear which, incidentally, is painted red, and the application of the later large size British Railways logo, which was only applied to two engines of this class, the other being No.67261 - the lion on the BR emblem on No.67281 is, you will note, wrong facing but this discrepancy was probably never corrected during the engine's remaining lifetime. Just behind the bunker of the locomotive can be seen the rear of a westbound coal train made up of the old NER 21-ton wooden hoppers which were rapidly being displaced by Shildon built steel hoppers of greater capacity. *C.Campbell.*

On the morning of Saturday 5th May 1962, locally allocated V3 No.67688 stands simmering on the road situated on the south side of the 'Pacific' shed. The lean-to building, behind the engine bunker, which housed the Gateshead breakdown crane and its support vehicles, was nicknamed 'Kells' cabin by footplate staff. The engine displays one headlamp above the smokebox door, which denotes 'Stopping Passenger', though in this case its alternative, 'Breakdown train returning from incident' seems totally appropriate, if a little belated. Nevertheless, a footplate crew are taking in a few minutes sunshine by the shed door. *I.Falcus.*

A typically smoky Gateshead scene on 14th April 1962. Once again we have the diesel with steam mix in the yard. This time A3 No.60083 SIR HUGO, of Heaton depot, and in 'final condition' with double chimney and German-style smoke deflectors is 'nosed' by English-Electric 1-Co-Co-1 Type 4 Diesel-electric D283. *I.Falcus.*

Gateshead locomotive works had ceased carrying out major repairs to locomotives in 1959, the end of a second stint from when the establishment was revived during WWII from a previous closure. Part of the building was originally Greensfield passenger station, the terminus at the eastern end of the Newcastle & Carlisle Railway. The three road building at the south-eastern corner of the site, was utilised by Gateshead (52A) engine shed for light repairs. Inside of the building, on 30th May 1964, V3 No.67690 was a resident together with four J27s and another V1/V3. The overhead travelling crane is one of those supplied by the Stockport crane makers Wharton's. *H.Forster.*

The Pacific shed at Greensfield was adjacent to the most westerly roundhouse. In 1956 a 70 ft diameter turntable was installed in the most easterly of the four roundhouses, at the same time that two of those roundhouses were re-roofed and had their internal layouts dramatically altered with the turntables being taken out and straight stabling roads being installed through the full length of the buildings. The installation of the large turntable in the easterly roundhouse enabled Pacific locomotives to be housed in the main shed building for the first time, albeit somewhat late in the depot's long and colourful history. However, from that time on, and with the demise of mainline steam workings for Gateshead's remaining Pacifics, greater numbers of other classes of steam locomotives were to be seen inside the Pacific shed - the inner sanctum was now open to all and sundry. On 5th October 1963, Gateshead K1 No.62024 and Doncaster allocated A1 No.60149 AMADIS, flank Heaton based V3 No.67620, which was still showing signs of having been specially cleaned the previous week for the RCTS *North Eastern Railtour*, part of which it hauled from Newcastle to Ponteland. *H.Forster.*

52B – HEATON

Situated in the east end of Newcastle, Heaton also had a stud of Gresley, Peppercorn and Thompson Pacifics and V2s for passenger turns. Mixed traffic turns were handled by K3s with V1/3 on empty stock workings. A collection of J39s and J27s were used for freight service, and the resident shunters were from classes J71, J72, J77 and J94, plus the two ES1 Bo-Bo electric locomotives for working on the Quayside branch. Today the only remains of Heaton shed is the turntable, which was moved fifty yards further north from its original site.

The short tracks at the western end of Heaton engine shed were known to enginemen as 'The Park'. Here, on 14th September 1962, we see a typical weekend scene of the period with ex North Eastern Railway Bo-Bo electric ES1 No.26500 - as restored to NER apple green in 1961 - taking a rest from its Quayside branch duties. Sister engine, No.26501, would have been at South Gosforth car sheds during it's break. Stabled - parked - with the ES1 are three Drewry Class 04 diesel mechanical shunters, including Nos.D2322 and D2334, which were relative newcomers to Heaton depot, having arrived in 1961 along with Nos.D2329, D2332 and D2339. The signal behind the electric locomotive controlled the Up main line, and this was affectionately known to local 'spotters' as 'Little Billy'. The 'dolly' signal, sharing the same post, controlled all departures from the Up yard. The electrified tracks in the foreground are the Heaton-Tynemouth section of the North Tyneside loop. *I.Falcus.*

Grubby, locally based J27 No.65832 stands at the western exit to Heaton shed on 11th April 1964, the Foreman's office stands behind the engine. Access to the shed was across a footbridge which was in full view of the offices and illegal 'spotters' trying to gain entry would be immediately ejected. This action was in fact for their own safety as the shed was in the fork of two third-rail electrified lines! However, at the time it seemed harsh treatment. Note the bag hanging from the 'water column' or rather 'water bridge' in this case, which ran the width of the shed building and was a somewhat easier and cheaper method of installing water facilities in the shed yard than the more traditional water columns fed by an underground supply. New England shed had a similar situation but there the water arrived at the tender via a gantry. *I.Falcus.*

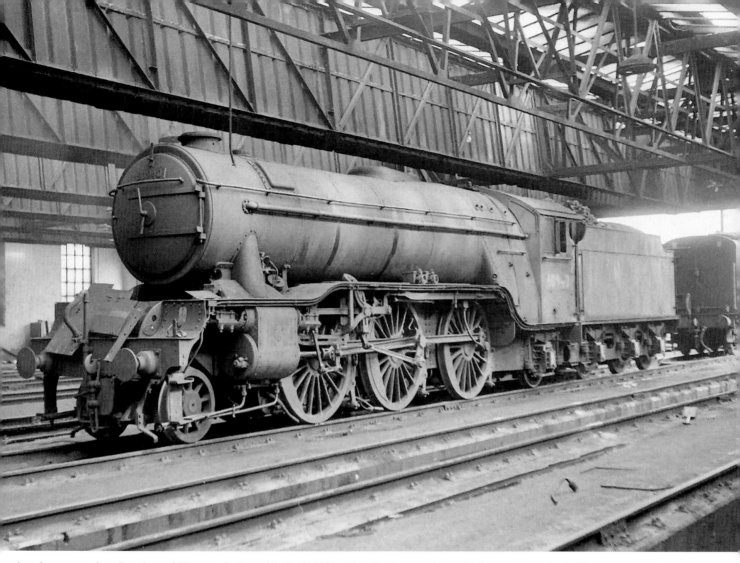

A rather sparse interior view of Heaton shed on 4th April 1964. Dieselisation on the main line was past the half-way stage at this time and the allocation of 52B was much reduced. At its home shed, V2 No.60940 is undergoing a repair to its middle cylinder which can be discerned by the cover plate lying on the front footplate; it is facing west in a virtually empty shed with only a Peppercorn A1 for company. Modellers - the asbestos clad smoke extracting duct channelling, with its angle-steel framing is worthy of note. *I.Falcus.*

This scene, at the eastern end of the shed on 28th February 1965, looks rather busy but is not what it seems. There is not a wisp of steam in sight. The nearest of the B1s, No.61167, is a stranger from faraway Canklow, where it was withdrawn, and is in transit to Hughes Bolckow at Blyth for scrap - note the motion is all intact and connected and as for the numberplate. Perhaps it travelled under its own steam, as sometimes happened, or it was towing other 'dead' locomotives to the same yard! The other B1 is No.61199, which was allocated to Tyne Dock shed at the time and was effectively on loan to Heaton for empty carriage workings which required winter steam heating. The A4, just visible inside the shed, is No.60027 MERLIN of St Rollox depot, under repair with its middle coupled wheelset removed. The Pacific worked home to Glasgow light engine a couple of days later. *I.Spencer.*

A fabulous photograph of Heaton V3 No.67652, taken 29th October 1961, at the east end of the shed. The tank is raising steam ready to reverse onto its empty stock in the carriage sidings in the far distance. What a wealth of detail is to be seen on this locomotive, just look at the front end alone: The North British destination board brackets, on the very top of the smokebox front ring, were fitted to all V1/3s. The four rivets below the smokebox numberplate secured the brackets which held the Great Eastern area destination boards, whilst the extra lamp brackets were for the NB section. What a shame one of these engines was not preserved. I remember six of them standing in Thompsons scrapyard at Stockton for quite a while; unfortunately before the preservation movement got really off the ground. *I.Falcus.*

A view dated 28th April 1957, showing A2 No.60539 BRONZINO, which spent most of its working life as a Heaton engine, apart from its last year, which was spent at Tweedmouth shed. Fitted with the rather ugly unlipped chimney, and contrary to popular opinion, I found rather attractive. The location is an area inside the depot called the 'dead-line' which was beyond the eastern end of the shed building. These roads were used to stable engines awaiting either shed attention or weekend stabling; in later years for storage became the main function here. The manual coaling stage can be seen on the left of the picture. *I.Falcus.*

On 12th April 1963, having just worked a train into Newcastle (Central) from the north, Tweedmouth A1 No.60151 MIDLOTHIAN has reversed onto the Heaton coaling stage, to keep company with a V3 2-6-2 tank. MIDLOTHIAN was a Darlington built engine denoted by the flush sided tender compared with the Doncaster batch, which had snap headed rivets. The water crane on the wall - note the attendant brazier sited immediately below - and the general decrepit state of the brickwork is worthy of note. *I.Falcus.*

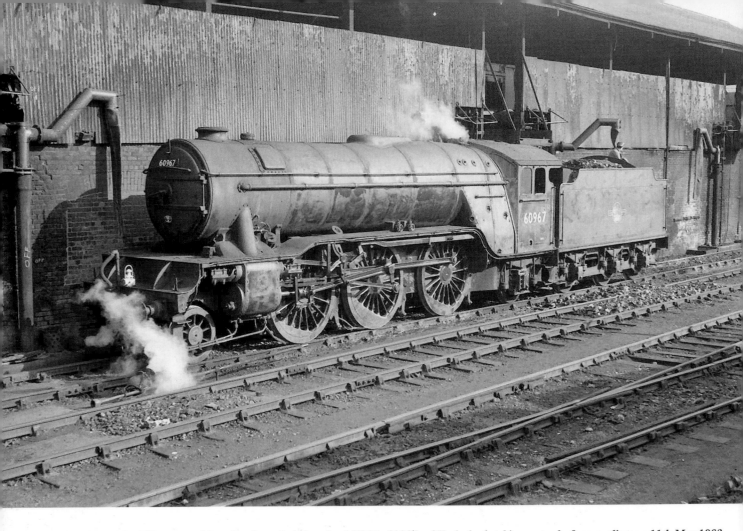

Another view of the 52B stage, with a nice shot of work-stained V2 No.60967, of York shed, taking water before coaling on 11th May 1963. This engine is coupled to a long cut-out Group Standard tender, with separate tool boxes. The fixing of corrugated iron cladding, which screened much of the stage coaling floor from the elements, especially the vicious easterly winds, was one of the concessions made to the coalmen who filled the wheeled tubs direct from the Loco. Coal wagons. When many areas of the LNER had mechanical coaling plants installed at their locomotive depots, the NE Area appears to have overlooked that aspect of steam locomotive servicing except at a few places, Selby, Leeds and York coming to mind. However, the NE Region followed the same route and kept hold of the manual coaling stage instead of mechanisation! Considering that Dairycoates virtually led the LNER Locomotive Running Department into mechanising the coaling process (and that with a huge plant erected by the North Eastern), it makes you wonder what happened to bring it to a virtual halt. Local practices, local trades, local jobs! *I.Falcus.*

(*opposite*) A very fine study of the publishers' namesake A3. Heaton depots A3 No.60088 BOOK LAW was still in its original form, when it was captured on film after it had just reversed to the eastern extremity of the shed yard, between the ash-pits and the coaling stage. This view was taken on 27th April 1958; the early Gresley Restaurant Car, on the extreme right, is still in crimson and cream (blood and custard) livery. *C.Campbell.*

52C – BLAYDON

This shed, standing to the west of Newcastle, on the south bank of the Tyne, was coded 52C. Gresley D49/2s from here were used on the Border Counties trains whilst G5 and V1/3 worked local passenger turns. A host of mixed traffic and freight engines from classes K1, J39, Q6, J21 took care of a variety of tasks. The shunting locomotives comprised engines from the ranks of classes J71, J72, and J94, together with a solitary N10. The six coupled tanks covered all of the work in the yards west of Newcastle (Central) station, on the north side of the Tyne, besides those to the west of Dunston Staithes on the south side of the river. The only remains of Blaydon engine shed today are the office buildings erected in 1957 on the north side of the yard. Given over to non-railway use, they had been occupied by the Co-operative Dairy until recently vacated.

According to LNER enginemen these are the engines that won the war! Residing on Blaydon shed on Sunday 20th July 1958, was V2 No.60860 DURHAM SCHOOL of Gateshead shed. The engine is coupled with the LNER Group Standard V2 tender, which had short cut-outs and integral toolboxs. Normally it was a York V2 which was serviced at Blaydon prior to returning home on a balancing working. The engine concerned having worked a York to Carlisle mixed goods train as far as Addison sidings, at the west end of Blaydon. We can only assume that the Gateshead locomotive has been borrowed by York on this particular occasion. *H.Forster.*

The siding next to the Chain Bridge Road at Blaydon was the regular stabling point for locomotives which worked the Border Counties line to Hawick. Duties were shared between Blaydon and Hawick sheds, in the early with D30s usually working the first southbound trains from Hawick to Newcastle (Central) whilst D49s from the Tyneside shed worked the first northbound trains and most of the return services throughout the day. The D30 worked an early evening service back to Hawick to get it home. In the 1950s, the Blaydon D49s were the most frequently used motive power on the line and handled three pairs of daily trains but the Hawick locomotives had to stable overnight at Blaydon on alternate days and at weekends. There was no Sunday service on the BC line, hence the reason why D49/1, No.62771 THE RUFFORD, was only in 'light steam' on Sunday 5th February 1956. The photographers' normal means of transport is the period bicycle, with a pedal propped against the kerb. Complete with saddlebag, dynamo and metal mudguards, it looks a fine machine and is in fact an Elswick Beaumont - built in Newcastle. *H.Forster.*

Here, in December 1950, we see austerely painted ex NER Class O, LNER G5 and now BR G5, No.67255 on the ash-pits at Blaydon shed. Keeping the 0-4-4T company, shortly before the G5's 1951 withdrawal, is resident J39 No.64852. Because of its fairly early demise, this particular G5 did not receive the full British Railways mixed traffic livery but it did have a 'claim to fame' in that it was 'called-up' for wartime service at the Royal Ordnance Factory at Bishopton, Renfrewshire from 1941 to 1944. *E.Wilson.*

Apart from the ten 9Fs at Tyne Dock shed, very few locomotives from the British Railways Standard classes were allocated to Tyneside sheds. On 20th of May 1956, resident Standard Cl.4 No.76047 was stabled on the yard at Blaydon shed for its next duty to Hawick. By now the days were over for the Blaydon D49s on the Border Counties line as these Standard Cl.4 muscled in. However, the line was to lose its passenger services six months hence so the work for these 2-6-0s was also slowly being eroded anyway. It may seem incredible but the Cl.4 was just thirteen months old when this picture was recorded. Having arrived at 52C from 52A during the previous October, the 'new' engine has obviously not had the benefit of a clean and was probably never likely to whilst on the Blaydon allocation. A month after this sad spectacle was presented, No.76047 packed its bags and transferred to Kirkby Stephen where it was at least appreciated for the next four years. I'm sure the advertising hoarding were put up to prevent the spotters seeing the engines - look at that rear side detail. *H.Forster.*

More Standards sharing the doom and gloom of post-war Britain. As the Cl.4s eluded to previously departed from Blaydon, a pair of Standard Cl.3s, Nos.77011 and 77014 arrived Blaydon shed, primarily to work on the Haltwhistle-Alston branch. Once again North Eastern Region contempt shone through the paintwork of these engine which, although just slightly older than the Cl.4s, they were nevertheless young locomotives in the great scheme. Initially No.77011 had gone new to Darlington in June 1954 but two months later it transferred to West Auckland from which depot it arrived at Blaydon. No.77014 also started life at Darlington but it moved to Whitby in November 1955 and from where it reallocated to Blaydon. After being serviced, No.77011 was awaiting its next duty at Blaydon shed on 17th June 1956. Apart from the Alston duty, the other Cl.3 locomotive was spare and was therefore used for a wide range of tasks varying from empty stock working from Scotswood Bridge sidings to Newcastle Central station, to working trains to Hawick during the last week of the passenger services in October 1956. Behind the wooden wagon on the left, we see one of Hawick's Standard Cl.2 78XXX tender engines. *H.Forster.*

Freight trains for the Tyne Valley line to Carlisle were assembled at Addison sidings at the west end of Blaydon. In the 1950s, and early 1960s, haulage was dominated by Blaydon's K1s and some of the Carlisle Canal K3s. Ten of the former locomotives, Nos.62021 to 62030, were delivered new from North British Locomotive Co. Ltd., during the latter part of 1949. These were later joined by Nos.62002, 62006 and 62010, which had originally been allocated to Darlington. The K1s total wheelbase was slightly longer than that of the K3s which had preceded them before the war. The K3s were uncomfortable on the 50ft diameter turntables in the double roundhouse at Blaydon so, like their predecessors, the Peppercorn K1s were kept in the open, and only occasionally could one be found with its tender protruding through the rear wall after having reversed over both turntables. No.62027 and a B1 standing on the former Border Counties locomotive road on 26th March 1961, were possibly awaiting attention from fitters. Sister K1 No.62028 is also stabled across to the left. *H.Forster.*

Having been withdrawn several days earlier but still carrying all of its plates, Heaton allocated B1 No.61241 VISCOUNT RIDLEY, is in a very run-down condition but otherwise wholly intact. Standing alongside the, by then, extremely decrepit coaling stage at Blaydon on 13th December 1962, the six-coupled mixed traffic locomotive awaits its fate. Condemned during a period of BR history which can only be described as something akin to a mass cull of steam locomotives, No.61241 had some waiting to do before an appointment with the scrapman. Eventually, during the following March, the call came and it was hauled to Darlington for that fateful last meeting. No stranger to Blaydon, this B1 had been allocated here during the previous two years, though under more auspicious circumstances. Even though a 52B shed plate is in place on the smokebox, the transfer to Heaton, in September 1962, may not have been wholly completed on paper by the time withdrawal took place hence the rather melancholy return to 52C. This engine spent most of its fifteen year long career at Tweedmouth, working the stopping passenger services to Newcastle and to Edinburgh. The external condition of the 4-6-0 probably had nothing to do with Heaton shed and more than likely the B1 arrived at that place already in this condition. It is difficult to realise that two months prior to its first 'arrival' at Blaydon in June 1960, it had just completed a General overhaul at Darlington works and during which event it was given a complete repaint, with full lining. Beyond the engine, the brick building elevating the water tank housed the sheds Blacksmiths shop. Beyond that was the western entrance to the roundhouse shed. Like all NER engine sheds, the space below the coaling stage was often utilised as accommodation for various shed trades and the rooms beneath the stage at Blaydon housed the Joiners shop, wood store, iron store, electric shop, Firedroppers, Ash fillers, and Platelayers. By today's standards, including industrial conditions found within the Emerging nations, those working and resting spaces were grim. *C.Campbell.*

28

Now preserved J21 No.65033 in the roundhouse at Blaydon during the mid-fifties complete with snow-plough. This engine spent many years allocated to Darlington and worked passenger trains over Stainmore to Kirkby Stephen, Tebay and Penrith. It transferred to Blaydon in 1951 when displaced by new LMS Ivatt designed 2MT 2-6-0 tender engines. At its new home, it was regularly sub-shedded at Reedsmouth for working the pick-up goods trains on the Border Counties line. It also became a regular engine for the popular summer Sunday outings known as the 'view the Station Garden' excursions from Newcastle to Bellingham, Rothbury and Morpeth. Late in life, the engine was called in to Darlington works and received a 'General' overhaul in late 1958. Through efforts made by the Railway Correspondence & Travel Society, the North-Eastern Region of British Railways agreed to run a railtour for the engine on 18th June 1959, the *STAINMORE LIMITED*, a 3-coach train from Darlington to Kirkby Stephen and Tebay, then on to Carlisle, returning via Penrith and Appleby. No.65033 saw further service from South Blyth on the weekly goods to Rothbury and West Woodburn, on the truncated line towards the Border Counties. Withdrawal took place in April 1962 but for an unexplained reason the engine remained at Darlington shed, supposedly for 'official' preservation. Time elapsed and as its condition deteriorated, the Curator of the new Industrial museum being set up at Beamish, arranged for the engine to be collected as a 'donation'. Now, 50 years after 65033's proudest moment there is, at last, hope of a full restoration. Ironically, as LNER 876, it was withdrawn in November 1939 and reinstated in December due to the prevailing wartime conditions! *H.Forster.*

A J71 extremely dirty and just recognisable as No.68273, had served for several years as Blaydon coaling stage pilot before being set aside with the prospect of little work in the future. It was seen at the side of the shed on 8th December 1956, less than twelve months prior to being withdrawn. Showing some nice detail of the wooden sandwiched bufferbeam, NER buffers and, in front of the cab spectacle plate and appearing like a candelabra - the fire iron trident - an implement which incidentally, was fitted to all NE tank engines. The engine shed facilities at Blaydon were quite modern when compared with most other comparable NER engine sheds. Opened in 1900, the stabling consisted two in-line 'square roundhouse' sheds, each with a 50ft turntable and twenty-four stabling stalls. Hydraulically operated sheer legs, built in iron, were installed in the shed next to the stores, workshop and general office. By the mid-fifties the shed roof was deteriorating rapidly so BR had a contractor patch with corrugated materials. At the same time the gable wall on the west end of the roundhouse was demolished and a new screen wall, with two entrance/exits was provided. The end for the depot was near and the place closed to steam in June 1963. Its then temporary role as a diesel depot lasted all of twenty-one months. A year later, in May 1966, it was demolished. Just sixty-six years had elapsed from completion of the facility to complete devastation. *H.Forster.*

The neat looking two-road sub-shed at Hexham, had recently been re-roofed and evidence of the contractors 'presence' is still around the site for all to see. North-Eastern sub-sheds had their own permanent allocations in steam days, before the arrival of diesel railcars from 1955. Hexham had six engines, during the period from 1950 to 1954, for passenger trains. These normally consisted two G5 0-4-4 tank engines, and two of the larger V1/V3s. For the goods duties, a J21 or J25 would work alongside a single J36. This view, taken 18th July 1954, shows G5 No.67320 with its nose sticking out of the rear (western aspect) of the rebuilt shed. This engine was later transferred away to Gateshead where its only diagram was a workman's train to Hartlepool, at 7-30 a.m. During its rebuilding, the shed managed to keep its original stone walls whilst a new roof was constructed from precast concrete section. The resultant marriage of concrete to stone left the ugly bund on top of the stone wall whilst on top of that a brick parapet was topped off with further precast segments. This particular engine shed had something of an unlucky past. In 1929 a fire destroyed the original (1878 built) roof. Almost immediately a new roof was constructed but a stray incendiary bomb, apparently dropped from a German aircraft in circa 1942 took that roof away too. In the background, Hexham East signal box dominates the skyline as it straddles the main line in NER fashion. "So, just where did you get that cornet?" "At the shop around the corner". *A.R.Goult.*

52D – TWEEDMOUTH

Coded 52D, and some sixty miles north of Newcastle - besides being the furthest shed away in the 52 district, Tweedmouth also had a two road sub-shed at Alnmouth. Here were outstationed D20s, provided for the Alnmouth to Alnwick and Alnmouth to Newcastle stopping trains. Tweedmouth itself had a small allocation of Pacific locomotives for main-line 'standby' duties. A good selection of mixed traffic engines consisting V2s, B1s and K3s worked the Edinburgh and Newcastle services, whilst in the early Fifties they had J39s, G5s and C15s for branch working. For general shunting work a couple of J72 and J77 tank engines sufficed. Today a substantial part of the depot remains intact - the roundhouse itself - housing small industrial units.

Passing loco coal wagons destined for the shed coaling stage, locally based G5 No.67268 runs round its Berwick-Kelso train at Tweedmouth in early 1955, just months before withdrawal. Though this reversal was an operating inconvenience, it proved invaluable after the 1948 floods when the non-stop FLYING SCOTSMAN could, at times run from Kings Cross to Edinburgh without stopping. Some of the passenger trains on the branch ran through to St Boswells and these produced an array of ex NBR engines from Hawick, such as D30 4-4-0s and C15 4-4-2 tanks. Tweedmouth often provided D20 4-4-0s and J39 0-6-0s. In latter days Class 2MT 2-6-0s, of both LMS and BR varieties, dominated. *C.J.B.Sanderson (Armstrong Trust).*

A typical scene inside a North Eastern roundhouse. Arranged around the turntable at Tweedmouth on 13th July 1953 were J39s Nos.64925 and 64941, both showing signs that they had been repaired at Cowlairs works by the inscribed TWEEDMOUTH on the bufferbeam, along with the painted edges of the smokebox numberplates. Sandwiched between them, J21 No.65070 looks diminutive. The well lit picture, admittedly captured inside a well maintained and clean shed, illustrates the cast iron columns supporting the roof and the smoke vents above the locomotives. Built in 1877, the roundhouse was equipped with a 45ft diameter turntable enabling locomotives such as these Gresley J39s to fit on comfortably. The four-road straight shed, built in 1847 by the Newcastle & Berwick Railway, housed the larger engines including the resident Pacifics. A larger turntable in the south-east corner of the yard, next to the roundhouse was used by the larger locomotives. After the depot closed in June 1966, the straight shed was demolished but the North Eastern built roundhouse was left intact. British Railways then utilised the roundhouse to store a number of pre-Grouping 'foreign' locomotives belonging to what was to become the National Collection. Its railway career over, the roundhouse took on a new lease of life in private use and has since housed various enterprises. Hopefully, the roundhouse might one day be recognised as an important component in the history of Britain's railways. *H.Forster.*

33

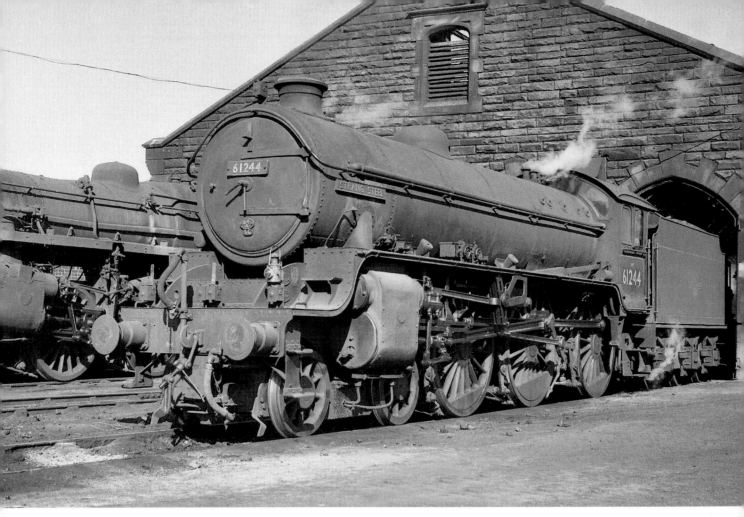

A lovely portrait, captured in December 1964, of St Margarets B1 No.61244 STRANG STEEL. Named after an LNER Northern Division Director, the B1 stands outside facing west, ready to take a freight back to Edinburgh; alongside is Tweedmouth Standard Cl.3 No.77002. The filled-in corners of the valancing, akin to most of the Scottish based B1s, is clearly visible. Tweedmouth's roundhouse, which stood behind the four-road straight shed, is one of the few steam era engine sheds still standing today. *C.J.B.Sanderson (Armstrong Trust).*

(*opposite, top*) St Margarets based D30 No.62424 CLAVERHOUSE rests on Tweedmouth shed yard on 5th June 1954, having just arrived on an excursion from Peebles. The burnt smokebox door was so typical of many Scottish engines being worked hard but this 4-4-0 seems to have been driven towards destruction, the shedplate is white and was probably all but welded to the door. The V2 on the left was probably the 'main-line standby' which the shed supplied continuously or on a 24/7 basis to use modern parlance. The K3s in the background were the workhorses of Newcastle-Edinburgh freights for years, the one on the extreme right is 52D's own No.61969. *C.J.B.Sanderson.*

(*opposite, bottom*) One of Tweedmouth's two allocated 'Antelopes' B1 No.61014 ORIBI (the other was No.61025 PALLAH), simmers in the yard on 30th May 1955. Like No.61241, seen earlier on Blaydon, this engine also had a lengthy spell on slow passenger workings to Newcastle and Edinburgh. The smokebox number plate was positioned at a higher level, indicating that the door originally belonged to an engine of the 61350-99 series. In the right background can be seen the 'standby' engines - an A1 and a V2. *F.W.Hampson (Armstrong Trust).*

A nicely turned out Gresley workhorse, J39 No.64813, stands on the ash pit alongside the repair shed at Tweedmouth on 5th June 1954. From the stopping passenger headcode, it is probable that the engine has just arrived from Eyemouth, this class was the mainstay of the branch for both the passenger and goods services for many years. The repair shed - shed seems highly inadequate in this case - dominating the background is a superb piece of architecture built mainly from dressed stone and with a high pitched slated roof. The rooflights, and indeed the ornate stone mullion windows, must have cast plenty of light (assuming they were clean) onto the job in hand inside this wonderful monumental edifice to steam era repair facilities. Note the walkway on the roof, leading, in this case, to hutted a trap door which allowed access to the top of the sheer legs. *C.J.B.Sanderson (Armstrong Trust).*

The classic lines of a superb mixed traffic locomotive, Tweedmouth's own K3 No.61901, on the ash-pits 5th June 1954. The engine standing in neutral gear, is waiting for the necessary to be carried out. This further aspect of the Repair shed shows the array of roof lights to the full along with the wooden steps leading to the small garden style tool shed masquerading as an entrance. Obviously ladders were required to reach the roof itself and these would no doubt be the preserve of the Outdoor Machinery Department when they came along for their annual, or whatever frequency of inspection was required. Window cleaning was obviously left to the elements but this dirtier than normal neighbourhood must have kept the rain busy. Even the finial atop the east gable had a grandeur about it which can only be marvelled at. *C.J.B.Sanderson (Armstrong Trust)*.

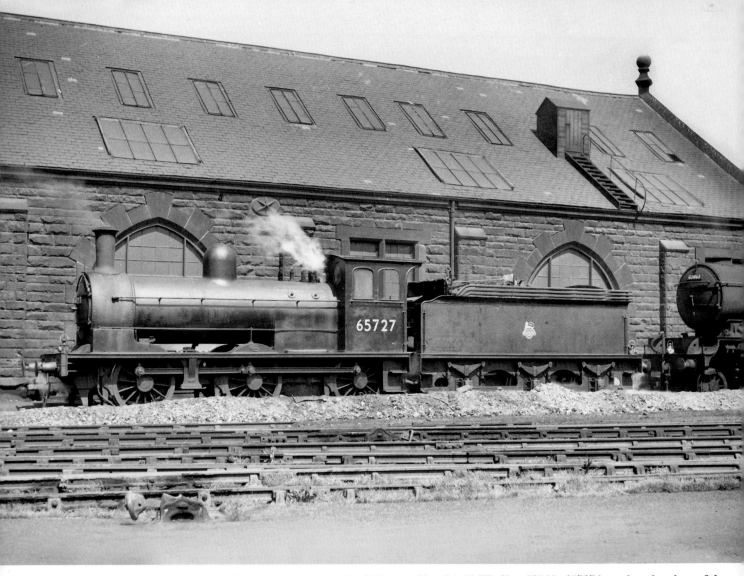

Taken on the same day as the previous illustration, we see ex North Eastern Class P1, LNER Class J25 No.65727 has taken the place of the K3 over the ash pits. Tweedmouth had two J25s in December 1950, the other being No.65697. *C.J.B.Sanderson (Armstrong Trust).*

(*opposite*) A rather unusual visitor inside Alnmouth shed, a sub of Tweedmouth, is Dundee based V2 No.60836. On Tuesday 31st May 1966, the V2 was commandeered from Tweedmouth shed after arriving on a railtour. It was then pressed into service and used on the Alnmouth to Alnwick passenger turns for a couple of days. This happened to be the last operational Scottish Region V2 and was subsequently withdrawn on New Years Eve 1966. *E.Wilson.*

52E - PERCY MAIN

The former Blyth & Tyne engine shed and associated workshops at Percy Main, British railways shed code 52E, was situated to the east of Newcastle, along the north bank of the Tyne. It had an allocation consisting entirely of J27 0-6-0s which were used mainly for colliery traffic, and later for oil trains serving the Esso terminal at East Howdon. Upon closure in 1965, the site was cleared and a council estate constructed in its place.

Backing southwards, towards Engine Shed Junction in early December 1964, J27 No.65813 is seen passing Percy Main shed. With brakevan in tow, the J27 is about to pick up a train at the Esso oil terminal to deliver fuel to the RAF base at Carlisle. This engine, bearing works No.18358, was one of twenty built for the North Eastern in 1908 by the North British Locomotive Company at its Atlas works in Glasgow, denoted by the circular brass plate affixed to the front splasher. The 0-6-0 has the normal 9in. x 5in. LNER/BR plate on its middle splasher. Note the inclined track on the other side of the bridge. This was the ramp for the depot's coaling stage. *G.Armstrong collection.*

The small complex of buildings at Percy Main were originally the works and engine shed of the Blyth & Tyne Railway, whose main source of revenue was generated by supplying motive power and wagons for use on the extensive coal traffic from the collieries to the B&TR staithes on the Tyne. A view of the through shed on 4th January 1959, looking north, shows the partially demolished shed, with its original three pitched roofs (one over each road) missing, along with the end gables which had arched entrances over each road. A crude lean-to was constructed over the eastern-most road in early 1956 for the benefit of the fitters working on the steam locomotives but no attempt was made by British Railways (NE Region) to cover the old running shed. This particular building was the original engine shed of the B&TR, the main works, being out of frame here, were just to the right of where the photographer was standing. Constructed beforehand but certainly in use by 1855, the running shed was built entirely of stone. It is northern end, the engine shed had what appeared to be a fourth road attached to its eastern side (the profile of that building can be gleaned from the gable next to the lean-to) but this was probably a workshop simply attached to the shed building at the time of erection or as a later addition. Certainly, and at least since Grouping, that building does not seem to have been used for locomotive purposes. Like many former NER engine sheds during the period depicted by the photograph, the place was a bit of a mess. The phrase '...knee deep in...' comes to mind as the ash and clinker builds up to axle level. Furrows are already being made in the pile between rails by bits attached to the engines. How much longer could the mess be allowed to grow? Also in view are a number of Percy Main's exclusive steam allocation of Class J27 locomotives; Nos.65842 can be seen on the left and 65809 to the right. *C.Campbell.*

Brand new Hunslet diesel-mechanical D2594, by the side of Percy Main's former repair shop, and in sight of the Foreman's office, 15th April 1960. During September and October 1956, Percy Main shed became the first BR establishment on Tyneside to embrace diesel maintenance - for shunters only - and 52E received a small allocation of BR Darlington built, 350 hp, 0-6-0s (later Class 08), D3316, D3317, D3321, D3322, and D3324. In May 1958 their ranks were swollen by the arrival of D3673, D3674, D3678, and D3679. Finally, in March 1960, Derby built examples of the same class appeared at 52E in the shape of D3938, D3939, D3942, D3943. In March 1959, three of the smaller, 204 horsepower, 0-6-0s (later Class 04) followed from Drewry Car Co. but built in the North East by Robert Stephenson, & Hawthorn; a fourth new one, D2321, turned up two years later from the same maker. A further 1960 event saw Doncaster built 204 hp. 0-6-0s (later Class 03) D2092 and D2093 arrive in June, along with D2149 from Swindon. Our friend here the solitary Hunslet type (later class 05), may not have been very successful at Percy Main as, after a trial period, it was re-allocated to Tweedmouth shed for duties around Berwick. The former repair shop, which appears to be well maintained in this view, was converted during 1956 for the housing and maintenance of the above diesel shunters hence the reason for the lean-to within the walls of the old steam shed. Note the mechanical extractors placed on the ridge of the diesel shop roof - all mod cons for these lads. One final point, the track on which the Hunslet diesel is standing inclines slightly below ground (yard) level just like, but not as deep as, the sunken ash roads once found at most exNER engine sheds. Was this an early form of ash road (they did not come into general usage on the NER until the early 1900s)? Surely locomotive servicing and all its associated filth was not carried out on this side of the works in the early days of the B&T. Answers, suggestions, ideas, etc., to the Publisher please. *I.H.B.Lewis.*

In the 1950s, prior to the arrival of diesel shunters in September 1956, Percy Main shed had an allocation made up entirely of Class J27. These extremely capable and reliable 0-6-0s were employed mainly on the transfer of coal from mines in south-east Northumberland to staithes on the River Tyne at North Shields and Dunston. From the Tyne, the coal was shipped to power stations in south-east England. Standing on the shed yard outside the three-road dead-end shed is local boy No.65796, coaled and ready for another days work removing vast amounts of Northumberland to the holds of coastal colliers. The three road building, with the two road repair shop along its eastern wall, was once part of the main workshop of the B&TR but was converted into a running shed by the NER at an unknown date. In the background beyond the front of the engine can be seen part of the depots 'oil farm' for the resident diesel shunters; a rail tank wagon masks part of the installation. Whereas the diesels had their fuel supply on the premises, the steam locomotives had to proceed off shed, negotiate various points on the 'main line' and steam south under a road bridge to the ramped coal stage. Admittedly, engines finishing their shifts would visit the stage prior to going on shed but nevertheless, the procedure was by no means straightforward. One of the photographers whose work appears in this album, Ian Falcus, was sitting in the cab of an already coaled J27 at Percy Main on 18th April 1959 when the 0-6-0 still retained its tall NE chimney and dome. *H.Forster.*

43

52F - NORTH & SOUTH BLYTH

The town of Blyth, north-east of Newcastle, had an engine shed on each side of the river - appropriately labelled North and South but sharing the same code. Both were predominately freight sheds serving the coal industry, the South shed's stud of J27s were competent performers. G5s dominated the local passenger trains, and ten J77s worked on both the north and south staithes. The stud of locomotives at the North shed was used primarily for coal traffic, with examples of classes J21, J25 but mainly J27s, the latter dominating the mineral haulage. Later, in the mid-sixties, redundant engines from other North Eastern sheds were transferred in, and these comprised classes K1, Q6 and Ivatt Cl.4. Both depots closed in 1967 and were later demolished, the site of the South shed now houses a small cottage hospital and the only remains of North Blyth shed is the Railway Institute building.

G5 No.67305, a lovely ex NER tank locomotive recently transferred from Darlington, where she had been a regular on trains to Middleton-in-Teesdale, stands outside the six-road South Blyth 'sub-shed' on 1st March 1958. This engine was push and pull fitted and was used on the branch to Monkseaton. Other members of the class worked the Blyth & Tyne 'main-line' from Newbiggin to Newcastle (Manors), whilst one engine, normally No.67296 was sub-shedded at Rothbury. *C.Campbell.*

Blyth's own J27 No.65795 was looking rather shabby as it peered out of the South shed building in August 1966 but the engine was already condemned and was simply waiting to be towed away for scrap. Note the state of the smokebox door which is either open and only slightly ajar, or is, more than likely, heavily distorted and perhaps the reason for its withdrawal. In the background, just inside the shed, is a sign of things to come around these parts in the shape of an English Electric Type 3 Co-Co diesel-electric (Class 37) hiding away from the sun. The general dereliction portrayed in this view shows that closure, which occurred in May 1967, was not far away. The position of the sun in this late morning scene indicates that the clock had stopped working too. *C.Campbell.*

The shedplate 52F denoted Blyth allocated J27s. Nos.65819 and 65814 were both appearing to be 'well looked after', as they stand together outside the South shed in the spring of 1966. Withdrawal came in October and June respectively, followed by a short journey to Hughes Bolckows at North Blyth and their demise in early 1967. These engines were the backbone of coal traffic motive power in Northumberland from North Eastern Railway days right up to the end of steam in 1967 - the vast army of NER 0-8-0s stayed firmly employed south of the Tyne. The South Blyth engine shed consisted six dead-end roads, but the shed had been constructed in two halves with the first three-road section, that which we are looking at now, opening in 1880. The other half came into operation during 1894. A 50ft hand operated turntable, situated between the shed and the main line, off to the left, sufficed throughout the lifetime of the depot. The coaling stage was, along with the various 'trades' spaces beneath was positioned at the east end of the yard, opposite the passenger station. *I.Spencer.*

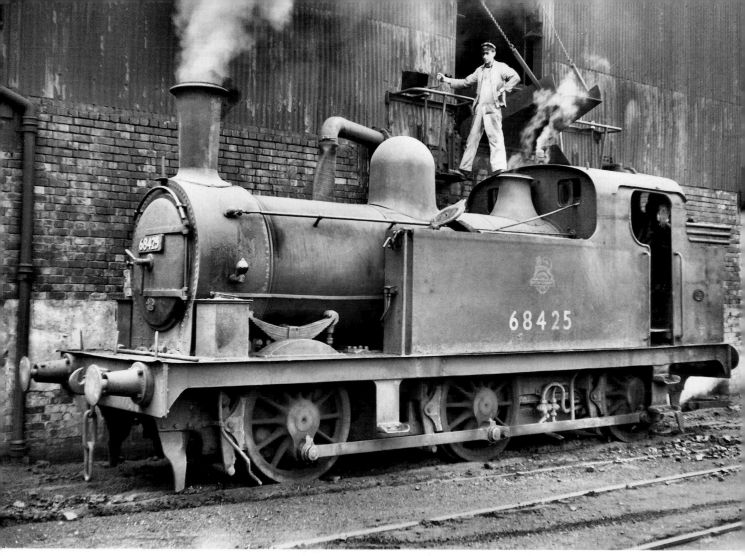

Ex NER Class 290, then LNER and BR Class J77, No.68425, had recently transferred from Darlington when photographed in February 1958, and still retaining a 51A shedplate. Taking water at the North shed coaling stage, the 0-6-0T was looking rather run-down and was probably living on borrowed time but what about the fireman in that precarious position! This engine, and several others of its ilk, shunted coal wagons onto the staithes. The J77 class were ideally suited for that purpose because of their power and ability to negotiate sharp curves when compared with other North Eastern 0-6-0 tank locomotives. Engines of this class were originally built as 0-4-4 welltanks of NER Class BTP for passenger use, but when large quantities of Worsdell Class 'O' 0-4-4 tank engines (LNER G5) were built at the turn of the century, many of the BTP class were rebuilt to 0-6-0 shunting tanks. No.68425 built at Darlington and subsequently rebuilt at York in 1904, lasted until 1960 - the fireman, hopefully, a damn sight longer! All the J77s rebuilt at Darlington had the standard NER cab fitted, whilst the York rebuilds retained their distinctive round-topped cabs. *B.D.Nicholson collection.*

(*opposite*) Inside the North shed roundhouse, August 1966. J27 No.65804 and another unidentified J27, together with two ex LMS Ivatt 4MT 2-6-0s, are probably all out of traffic. This interior scene of a roundhouse and similar shed environments, are now all in the past. What a shame, no more schoolboy memories of those lovely evocative smells, of steam, smoke, sooty wood and grease, can be found on the national rail network today. *C.Campbell.*

Fourteen minutes past one. Sunday 10th April 1965. Peppercorn K1s, Nos.62022 and 62024, in a rather run-down condition, stand on the east side of North Blyth engine shed. The roundhouse here was constructed in 1896 and opened for business the following year. All the usual facilities, including ramped coaling stage and an elevated water tank were provided. Inside the roundhouse a set of wooden sheerlegs completed the repair requirements for the depot's allocation, besides that of the South shed, when necessary. Being hand operated, the sheerlegs required lots of muscle so their use was 'restricted' - for want of a better word - but by 1930 the LNER had condemned them, much to the relief of the resident fitters. On a lighter note, we can see in the background, the staithes and cranes of a busy seaport. In the foreground, the sleeper fencing, so common to many railway installations and engine shed boundaries, gives away numerous clues as to its former 'occupation'. Regarding the K1s, a number of the class, which had seen service at Fort William, Blaydon, Darlington and March, ended their days working coal trains to and from the Blyth and Tyne area on traffic for which they were not designed. Both these engines would end up in the scrap yard at Hughes Bolckows, just across the roof, (not literally). *I.Spencer.*

Looking into the back yard of the Blyth roundhouse, from the north staithes on 22nd December 1964, we see a Q6, another type which, in earlier days, was seldom seen at Blyth. As eluded to earlier, the 0-8-0s rarely worked over the lines north of the Tyne, however, a few engines displaced from south side depots, such as Blaydon and Borough Gardens, found their way here near the end - to a temporary sanctuary perhaps! Q6 No.63359, with a part folded and rolled tarpaulin (employed to keep out the ravages of the cold northern winters when running tender first) draped over its cab roof, is in the company of local K1 No.62002. Sections of this roundhouse were condemned during 1966 and although certain stalls were suddenly 'out-of-bounds', such problems did not hasten the shed's demise because it was all set for September 1967 anyway. So what's a little inconvenience such as that, in the great scheme anyway? *I.Spencer.*

52G – SUNDERLAND

The engine sheds coded 54 after Nationalisation became part of the 52 group in 1958, so Sunderland changed from 54A to 52G. The depot's allocation was a mixture of passenger and freight engines; a good stock of G5s, and A8s for services to Newcastle, South Shields and Durham, where a couple of G5s were out-stationed for banking duties. J27s and shunters from J72 and J94 classes completed their allocation. Latterly Q6 and WD 2-8-0s help out during the final couple of years. Closed at the end of steam in the North-East, the roundhouse was demolished, whilst the straight shed was used to stable diesel locomotives until final closure in the 1990s - the site has now been cleared.

A cracking shot of four J27s, including Nos.65855, 65879 and 65811, are visible inside the roundhouse at Sunderland in 1966. Notice the patch on the tender of No.65811, besides the dents and blemishes in the boiler cladding. In latter days, Sunderland's engines were kept surprisingly clean, no doubt helped by the many photographers who visited the area to make their record on the extremely arduous inclines on the Silksworth Colliery branch. *B.D.Nicholson collection.*

Push and pull fitted G5 No.67338, outside the 'staggered' four road straight shed at Sunderland, 12th April 1957. At this time, diesel multiple units on local passenger trains were still in the minority and the G5s were still kept very busy. Those at Sunderland shed worked to Newcastle, West Hartlepool and Durham, the latter had a sub-shed where two G5s were kept, one of which was used for banking southbound main line expresses out of Durham. A further duty was on the Sunderland - South Shields branch which required a 'push and pull' fitted engine such as No.67338 here. Besides its half of a 'threepenny-bit' shaped roundhouse, 52G had two, two-road straight sheds which were built separately and at different times between 1857 and 1861. Both sheds, which were in fact one with staggered front and rear aspects, were re-roofed by British Railways in 1954 using the tried and tested segmented, pre-fabricated, concrete method which had been employed throughout the country since just before W.W.II. Although less than three years had elapsed since completion of the job, the resident locomotives have certainly done their best to give the new construction that aged look. The men on top of the J27s tender may have been discussing Sunderland FC's league position - which was probably near the bottom! *C.Campbell.*

Brewing up and ready for the off in April 1957. A8 Pacific tank No.69857 stands in the yard outside the westernmost straight shed at Sunderland depot, in a spot parallel to the previous photograph. These engines performed similar duties to the G5s - mainly suburban passenger and medium distance stopping trains. When the diesel multiple units eventually took over those passenger services from Sunderland's steam fleet in 1959, there cropped up a classic case of the Maintenance Department not knowing of the Operating Department's plans. Strangely, three of these large tank engines had just arrived back at Sunderland from Darlington works after heavy overhauls, whilst, at the same time, the A8 diagrams were declared redundant! The three A8's, in newly repainted and immaculate condition, were sent away and put into store at Borough Gardens shed. After about eighteen months lying idle at Gateshead's former but now closed freight locomotive depot, and with no prospect of the trio finding work anywhere, they were all sent off to Darlington works again but this time for scrapping! *C.Campbell.*

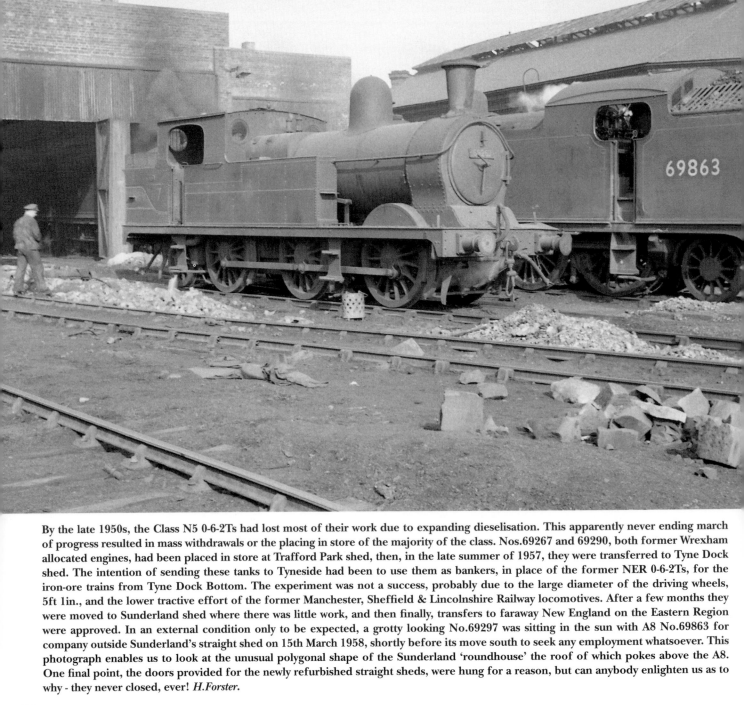

By the late 1950s, the Class N5 0-6-2Ts had lost most of their work due to expanding dieselisation. This apparently never ending march of progress resulted in mass withdrawals or the placing in store of the majority of the class. Nos.69267 and 69290, both former Wrexham allocated engines, had been placed in store at Trafford Park shed, then, in the late summer of 1957, they were transferred to Tyne Dock shed. The intention of sending these tanks to Tyneside had been to use them as bankers, in place of the former NER 0-6-2Ts, for the iron-ore trains from Tyne Dock Bottom. The experiment was not a success, probably due to the large diameter of the driving wheels, 5ft 1in., and the lower tractive effort of the former Manchester, Sheffield & Lincolnshire Railway locomotives. After a few months they were moved to Sunderland shed where there was little work, and then finally, transfers to faraway New England on the Eastern Region were approved. In an external condition only to be expected, a grotty looking No.69297 was sitting in the sun with A8 No.69863 for company outside Sunderland's straight shed on 15th March 1958, shortly before its move south to seek any employment whatsoever. This photograph enables us to look at the unusual polygonal shape of the Sunderland 'roundhouse' the roof of which pokes above the A8. One final point, the doors provided for the newly refurbished straight sheds, were hung for a reason, but can anybody enlighten us as to why - they never closed, ever! *H.Forster.*

One of the last depots to retain steam workings in the North-East was Sunderland (along with North Blyth and nearby West Hartlepool). As a result of this, several former Tyneside allocated locomotives ended up there, including a handful of Tyne Dock very own Q7 0-8-0s. There was still plenty of work heavy freight locomotives hauling the then vast amounts of coal from the deep mines on the eastern side of the Durham Coalfield. On 26th March 1961, Q7 No.63469, with a shunters pole protruding through the front frames in classic NER/LNER/BR style, was pictured alongside K3 No.61884. Having already started its third year of residence at Sunderland, Nos.63463, 63464, 63466, 63467, 63473 and 63474 were also there, No.63469 moved back to Tyne Dock in late August 1961. Now bearing in mind that the Westinghouse pumps had been removed from the engine in November 1959, there did not seem much point in the transfer but it took place anyway. In November 1961 the eight-coupled giant then attended Darlington works to be fitted with the AWS system (as were all the class at this time), but less than a year later the engine was condemned! Yes, and so was the rest of the class. They were interesting times when anything could and usually did happen. So, why was the Heaton based K3 on Sunderland shed? The 2-6-0 was resting prior to working a parcels van train from the Brian Mills catalogue warehouse at Hendon, which was closely situated to Sunderland shed. *H.Forster.*

Gresley J39 No.64701, was another refugee from Tyneside. The six-coupled engine had previously been gainfully employed, for several years, on trip workings between the various yards and goods depots on both sides of the River Tyne, after having been displaced at Blaydon in 1949 by the influx of new Peppercorn K1s which took over its duties on the Addison sidings to Carlisle London Road goods trains. The J39 arrived at Sunderland in December 1959 with Nos.64700, 64703, and 64704. Later, several other members of the class found their way to Sunderland too, the Group Standard tender of another can be seen on the right whilst at the rear, a BR Standard Cl.4, No.76024, was catching the warm rays of the morning sun when photographed on 26th March 1961. By now of course, serious inroads had been made into Class J39 by the scrapman but this particular locomotive was ensured a further eighteen months employment before condemnation. The amazing versatility of the Gresley 0-6-0 - they were happy on virtually any type of working, passenger or freight and were accepted everywhere too - would have given it a longer lifespan than that which actually took place but their demise was both swift and ruthless. Between May 1959 and December 1962 all the lot had gone bar a lone engine in Stationary Boiler use until late 1964 when it too was broken up. Not a trace of the 289 class members remain, anywhere. *H.Forster.*

With the departure of the G5s and A8s, from Sunderland shed, there was still a requirement to provide motive power to bank southbound East Coast main line trains which had stopped at Durham. This was, of course, a Sunderland duty, as also was the provision to move trains of parcels vans between Tyneside and Wearside. As a result, three V1/V3s were transferred into the depot for that work and pictured at Sunderland on 26th March 1961 was V3 No.67645, in the company of ex Percy Main 350 h.p., BR Darlington-built 0-6-0 DE shunter, D3678; note the small D as applied to the diesel at North Road works when new in August 1958. The V3 had initially arrived at Sunderland from Gateshead in September 1958 as a V1. However, in June 1959, it moved back to Tyneside but to Heaton shed instead. Just over three months later it was transferred back to Wearside prior to visiting Darlington for conversion to V3 class. In July 1962, with the banking job at Durham all but finished, the V3 returned to Heaton where it saw out 1962. During the first month of 1963 Gateshead got it back and it was at that depot where No.67645 was condemned in September 1963. Having spent most of its life in the North-East and all of it in former NER territory, the 2-6-2T was cut up at Darlington in October 1963, aged twenty-eight years. Its diesel companion here, as 08516, managed to surpass that by some margin. *H.Forster.*

A year before closure of the shed, a Sunderland Q6, No.63437, and K1 No.62008, of Darlington, were pictured outside the roundhouse, on 14th May 1966. The latter engine appears to have been on local shunting duties, as shown by a shunter's pole above the buffer beam but those engines working into the collieries with empties and taking out full loads over a distance of thirty miles or so would often carry a pole in this manner. To the left of the picture, all four roads of the straight shed can be seen as being empty, and although the shafts of sunlight make the building appear roofless, the light was actually shining through the glass fitted into the roof some twelve years previously during the rebuilding. Post-war plans envisaged nearly two million pounds being spent on a number of locomotive sheds in the NE Area but as we all know that money did not materialise and much of the work was not carried out. Sunderland, at least, got its rebuilt straight shed at a cost of £28,000 but more was to follow: mechanical coaling plant, wet ash pits and associated yard layout. Even the roundhouse was to get a new roof and a larger turntable was to replace the resident 42ft effort it had to make do with until the end. Sunderland however, was only in the second tier of this great scheme. Certain depots, such as Blaydon, Borough Gardens, Gateshead and Heaton, were in the top tier of priorities and expense, the plans for those places envisaged radical changes which were quite 'Thornaby like' in principal. But, as we now know, things worked out quite differently and priorities suddenly changed. Looking back, it might seem to have been something of a miracle that Thornaby was actually completed at all but its 'planned future adaptation for diesel locomotives' ensured its construction and commissioning by BR. As for Sunderland, well we can dwell on what the place might have looked like had steam remained 'king' and inflation had been better controlled. What we have here is the real image of the place as it neared its end. After steam was evicted in September 1967, the roundhouse was demolished but our old friend, the rebuilt straight shed, housed a small fleet of diesels for another twenty years or so - BR making sure they got back some return on their 1954 investment. Now about the cost of those three A8s !!!! *R.Stevens.*

52H - TYNE DOCK

Situated between Gateshead and South Shields, Tyne Dock shed was coded 52H and, as can be gleaned from its allocation, was purely a freight shed with a stud comprising Q6, Q7, Thompson O1, J21, and J25. WD 'Austerity' 2-8-0s and air-pump fitted BR Standard 9F 2-10-0s, for use on the Tyne Dock to Consett iron-ore trains, listed the tender engines. A stock of tank engines, provided for local workings, came from classes J71, J72, J94, and N10, with a solitary massive T1 4-8-0T completing the picture. The area where the shed stood and served the local railways for one hundred and five years, was cleared after closure and is now a humble housing estate.

Tyne Dock was also responsible for providing an N9 0-6-2T at Pelton Level, which was used to transfer loaded coal wagons from the end of the NCB Craghead branch to the Waldridge Incline from where they descended to Stella Gill sidings, South Pelaw, near Ouston junction. N10s replaced N9s following the withdrawal of No.69429 in July 1955. In the modernisation programme a 350 hp 0-6-0 diesel shunter replaced the N10. On 15th September 1957, No.69105, was spare engine in Tyne Dock roundhouse accompanied by J71 No.68262. The 0-6-2T is nicely embellished, amongst other things, with a silver painted thistle, probably by a driver with Scottish roots who also had a skill with the brush. *H.Forster*

Tyne Dock was a fairly large and important depot which in post-war years housed the entire class of Raven NER T3 0-8-0s (LNER Q7). These locomotives were mainly used on trains of iron-ore which they worked over the steeply graded line to the steelworks at Consett. The arrival of a fleet of new air operated side-door discharge bogie hoppers in 1950, allowed heavier loads to be carried and, as a result, five O1 2-8-0s arrived at Tyne Dock to share the arduous workings with the Q7s. The five O1s and five of the Q7s were fitted with Westinghouse air pumps for automatic ore discharge. The new, heavier, trains required one train engine and a banker out of Tyne Dock Terminal for about half a mile, then a further banker for about three miles from South Pelaw to Annfield Plain. A 'merry-go-round' loop was built at Consett - before such things became the norm at power stations - to enable the speedy turning of trains. Three separate wagon sets were built for the service and at times, nine return trains ran each day. Here, outside the Fitting shop at Tyne Dock, on 11th April 1957, is Thompson O1 No.63760 fitted with the twin air pumps. The photograph clearly shows the unusual standpipe on the front bufferbeam. Directly below the pumps, under the footplate on both sides, hung auxiliary air cylinders for operating the pumps; also very noticeable is the ex Great Central tender with which all the O1s were fitted. This view shows the differing levels of the valancing between the engine and tender. Ten BR 9F 2-10-0's took over the trains in 1958 until the end of steam working in 1965. *C.Campbell.*

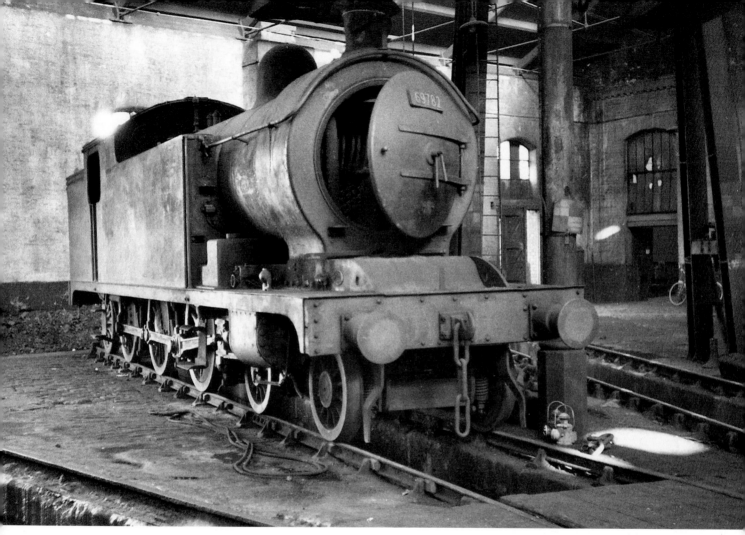

The banking of the loaded iron-ore trains from Tyne Dock Bottom, from 1953 when the new terminal was opened, and high capacity wagons were introduced, was initially trusted to T1 class 4-8-0Ts. However, when T1 No.69914 was withdrawn in 1955, it was not replaced by another of its kind. Instead, an A7 class Pacific tank, No.69782, transferred in from Hull to fill the vacancy. It would seem that the A7 was not a success, and so the die was cast for an assortment of different locomotive classes to be drafted in and tried out on the job. No.69782 was pictured, out of service, in one of the three Tyne Dock roundhouse on 13th November 1956. The hydraulic sheerlegs next to the locomotive should be a clue as to which shed this was but, to drop uncertainty into the mix, Tyne Dock had three sets of sheerlegs in all, two in the slightly larger No.1 roundhouse with its 50ft turntable, whilst the other stood in the north-west corner of the southern-most shed which was No.2. I'm batting for the latter because by the early Fifties the No.1 roundhouse was apparently roofless. The open doorway led out into the back yard where the coal stacks once stood; the doorway on the right went to the 'Kelbus' sand drier. Anyone who visited the place, and that apparently includes everyone who went there because, locally at least, you were regarded as a 'failed trainspotter' if you could not get around Tyne Dock shed. But, to get to the point, this area would be known by many, perhaps. The apparent pile of, whatever it is, leaning against the wall might well have been an outcrop of rock with the brick wall built directly onto its top surface? Maybe it was a pile of accumulated ash, clinker and dirt awaiting removal. Answers please. Well, you know the drill. *H.Forster.*

The five road straight shed at Tyne Dock was originally built to house steam railcars, and whilst the centre road leads into the No.3 and No.2 roundhouse, the other four roads dead-end as seen here. Three BR Standard 9F 2-10-0s, Nos.92062, 92098 and 92061, stand at the back of this shed on 24th May 1966. Tyne Dock shed had ten of these 9Fs, each fitted with twin Westinghouse air pumps for operating the bogie hopper doors on the Consett iron-ore trains. A job they had taken over from the eight-coupled Raven Q7 and Thompson O1 classes originally provided and equipped for the service. Note the hose from the water hydrant and connected to a centrifugal pump to give the water pressure a boost for washing out locomotive boilers. *R.Stevens.*

Recently ex works 9F No.92066 stands in the shed yard on 3rd November 1962, awaiting its next turn of duty. Although the picture is of the left side of the engine, whilst the pumps were on the right, we can actually see the auxiliary air tank hanging beneath the running plate; also the associated pipework. The original drawing show two cylinders being carried but only one was fitted, and on this side of the engine, free from the clutter around the area of the pumps on the right side. Reputedly the worst steamer of all the Tyne Dock 9Fs, according to Driver Gillis, it is perhaps understandable that No.92066 was the first to be withdrawn - 23rd May 1965. Though it was then sold to G.Cohen, at Cargo Fleet, Middlesbrough, it was actually cut up by Ellis Metals, at Swalwell, Gateshead. *I.Falcus.*

The roundhouse in this photograph, No.1, lost its roof in the early fifties (although it was the youngest of the three), and this view from 5th October 1963, taken from the footplate of a Q6, shows a further four members of the class Nos.63358, 63377, 63389 and 63453 plus a 9F tender grouped around the turntable. The latter appliance was not large enough to turn a 9F and the only reason that 9F is inside the place is because it is stabled on the through road which projected into the rear yard where the coal was stacked. Ahead of the Q6 from which the photograph was taken, stands the hydraulic sheerlegs which have been enclosed in a specially built corrugated shelter since this roundhouse had lost its roof. The roof in the centre background is that of the straight shed which at some time before 1880 was a roundhouse opened in 1862. The dilapidated roof in the right background belongs to the No.2 roundhouse, the two openings in the dividing wall allowing access and exit via No.1 shed if the single road through the straight shed was blocked. Before the advent of the 9Fs at Tyne Dock, five of the shed's own Q7s were fitted with the Westinghouse air pumps: No.63465 had one on each side of the smokebox, whilst Nos. 63460, 63463, 63469 and 63473, had them at the front end of the firebox, one each side. The O1s, it will be noted (see page 60) had them placed together on the right side of the firebox. Each pump served a different function; one opened the doors on the bogie hopper wagons, the other kept them closed. On the 9Fs the pumps were also placed together on the right side of the engine, again just forward of the firebox. Both the Q7s and the O1s required vacuum ejectors to be fitted to work the brakes on the new bogie hopper wagons. *F.Coulton.*

64

52J - BOROUGH GARDENS

Situated virtually in the centre of Gateshead, Borough Gardens was a freight depot situated directly one mile east of the parent depot and consisted four in-line square roundhouses, providing for the allocation of B1s, Q6s, J25, J27, J39s and shunters from classes J71, and J72. This shed also provided a home for many stored engines surplus to requirements during the winter months - A8s, D20s, G5s and V1/3 were regularly tucked-up there. When closed in 1959, the depot was demolished and Park Lane NCL Depot was constructed on the site. Here again storage prevailed when the new Tyne and Wear Metro units arrived they were also stored there. The site is now derelict.

The large four turntable roundhouse at Borough Gardens mainly housed Q6 0-8-0s, J25 and J39 0-6-0s and J71 along with J72 0-6-0 tanks and, curiously, three Thompson B1 4-6-0s which, for many years, had nocturnal freight workings to York and Stockton. The shed also was used for storage and members of classes B16 4-6-0, D20 4-4-0, J39 0-6-0, G5 0-4-4T, A8 4-6-2T and V3 2-6-2T had spells there. This May 1959 photo shows engines left to right as J71 No.68278, J39 No.64936, J72 No.69017, J27 No.65847 and J72 No.68695. What a fine array of smoke extraction units, wood, steel and trumpet shaped. The iron work supporting the roof is also worthy of note. *P.J.Robinson.*

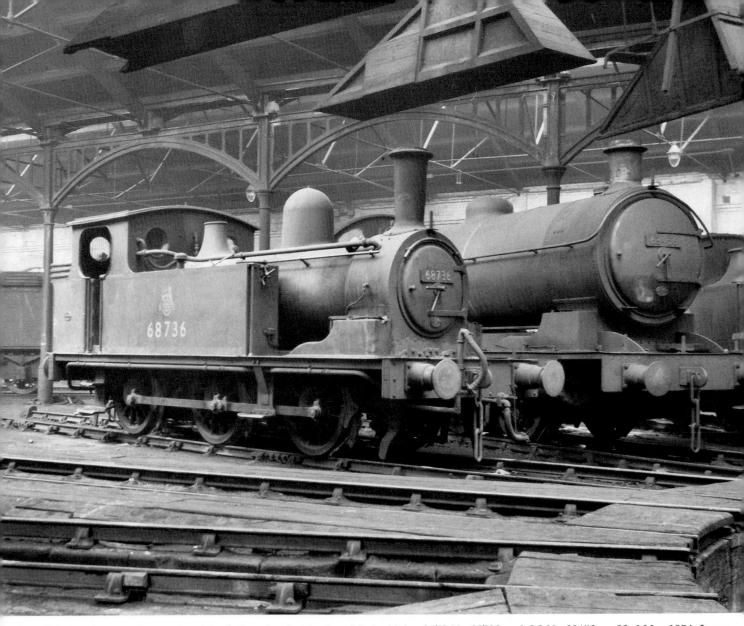

This interior roundhouse view (also believed to be Nos.1 and 2 sheds) is of J72 No.68736 and Q6 No.63456 on 23rd May 1954. It was taken before The J72 was transferred away to Starbeck and then to York, where it was repainted into North Eastern green livery for station pilot duties. When no longer required, No.68736 was, at the suggestion of North Eastern branch members of the RCTS, transferred to Tyneside to join green liveried No.68723 at Gateshead shed in July 1961. From there, the pair were utilised as Newcastle (Central's) station pilots. The illustration on the previous page was also probably captured in the Nos.1 and 3 roundhouses because the supporting ironwork, arching between the cast-iron columns is also cast-iron. By the late 1890s, when No.3 and 4 sheds were being constructed, rolled steel girders or lattice steel joists were being used as supports. *F.W.Hampson (Armstrong Trust)*.

A superb illustration of Borough Gardens wonderfully curved coaling stage in the summer of 1959, with a line of Q6 0-8-0s queuing for replenishment. This late afternoon view reveals No.63402 following No.63400. Worthy of note are the different tender coal rails and the new 52J shed code. The coal in those days was still a firemans delight, rather than the small 'duff' with which so many others had to shovel. The coal stage itself is a modellers delight and would certainly make a good prototype subject in any scale. Behind the coal stage we can just make out the roof of the No.1 and No.2 roundhouses, the first two of the four eventually built here. The roundhouses 1 and 2 were constructed for opening in 1875. No.3 and No.4 roundhouses, opened in 1898, stood in the same north-west/south-east alignment but north of the earlier pair making it possible to drive an engine from No.1 shed to No.4 shed, over four turntables and without leaving the interior of the sheds. *C.J.B.Sanderson (Armstrong Trust).*

The ash pits at 54C were located on one of the tracks leading into No.2 roundhouse, where a rather plain but attractive J25, No.65700, can be seen waiting for attention with Q6 No.63434 on 26th May 1956. Behind the engines can be seen a large but rather untidy supply of locomotive coal which was typical at most engine sheds in the days of steam. Note the temporary re-roofing being carried above the Q6. You could ask yourself why so much money was spent on engine shed repairs during this period in BR's history in what may appear to be a wasteful manner but remember that even though the Modernisation Plan had been announced in 1955, the following four years, at least, could be looked upon, perhaps, as the 'Age of Uncertainty' when local management still spent their budgets. Of course, this particular establishment was up for some serious rebuilding according to Post-war plans but the patching of the roof appears to have been the only money spent on the place as the same old methods of ash disposal and coal loading persisted to the end in 1959. *C.J.B.Sanderson (Armstrong Trust)*.

A rather strange visitor in the stabling area of Borough Gardens shed on Sunday 13th September 1953 is Sunderland allocated G5 No.67344. Normal visits for G5s, usually for storage, were in No.2 roundhouse, next to the Foremans office, which had the Shedmasters office above it. The stabling area, just east of the roundhouses, was necessary here to accommodate some of the depots larger residents and visitors. The turntables amounted to two of 42ft 6in. diameter and two of 45ft diameter - great for 0-6-0s but anything larger stayed outside so why was the G5 here? The tracks in the foreground lead from No.1 shed and were the only means of entry and exit for locomotives, other than using the turntable of No.2 shed for an exit/entry over the ash roads. It must have been horrendous for local housewives on washing days, living so close to a steam shed. *F.W.Hampson* (*Armstrong Trust*).

52K – CONSETT

The last member of the 52 shed group, was situated approximately twelve miles south-west of Newcastle. Its stud of locomotives in the Fifties consisted of Q6s for handling the coal and scrap traffic for the nearby steel works, and a couple of N8s for working the passenger trains to Newcastle. The engine shed buildings survived into the 1990s, albeit devoid of trackwork, but succumbed to the bulldozers when the whole site was landscaped leaving not a trace of the railways or the steel industry in the town.

Standing to the south of Consetts' two road engine shed, in March 1964, was what appeared to be a vast array of motive power, six Q6s with No.63345 to the right, and the remainder unfortunately unknown. Note the coaling crane just above the left hand Q6. These appliances were fairly common during the early years of the LNER but to see one at this late date, and operational, was quite rare. Look at all of that scrap metal in the background below the corrugated sheds, obviously destined for the furnaces of the steel works. *P.J.Robinson.*

A nice panoramic view of Consett's two road engine shed, yards and iron works, what a wealth of detail is incorporated in July 1963 picture. Loaded 16T minerals, 21T hoppers, plate wagons, brakevans, diesel shunters and in the foreground Q6s headed by No.63359 and K1 No.62050. Behind these is a selection of Consett Iron Company rolling stock, showing some of its crucible wagons and locomotives. The skyline is dominated by a vast conglomerate of its buildings and chimneys. The small BR engine shed blends somewhat into the background but nevertheless consisted just one building, built in 1875, until BR added another road in 1950. *B.Longstaff.*

52J - SOUTH GOSFORTH

The car sheds here, which housed the Tyneside electric units and diesel multiple units, became 52J in 1970 so was not associated with the main stream steam motive power depots except by code and then by some three years after their demise on the NE Region. In 2009, the depot still stands for servicing and housing the Tyne & Wear Metro units.

The two North-Eastern Bo-Bo electric shunters specially posed together outside South Gosforth depot for observation from a passing RCTS railtour. These engines, which were both third-rail and pantograph fitted, were repainted in NER green at an RCTS request, following the successful painting of station pilots No.68723 and 68736. Previously, these electric's had been kept in a grimy black livery making it difficult for 'spotters' to identify which was which. Designed for operating on the freight branch in Newcastle from a point just east of Manors stations, down to the Quayside, these locomotives were ideally suited for the steeply graded line with its tunnels and sharp curves. Current was supplied by overhead collection. One engine worked the Quayside branch from 06.00 Mondays until 12 noon on Saturdays. When not in use, the branch engine was positioned alongside the main line next to the tunnel entrance, and spent the weekends outside Heaton shed (see earlier illustration on page XX). Its first duty on each working day was to tow the steam pilot down to the Quayside and then bring it back on the final trip of the day. This was a J71 and later a J72, with the last built example, No.69028, being a regular choice. The other electric was kept at South Gosforth as spare, but sometimes shunted wagons bringing supplies to the depot, but it did not get involved with moving the EMUs because of their automatic couplings. Engines changed duties fortnightly. The EMUs in the background are Gresley 1938-built articulated sets supplied for the North Tyneside section in 1937/38, and lasted until the abandonment of electrification in 1967. South Gosforth received its first DMUs in 1955 and had a sizeable allocation until 1979 when the depot was transferred to the Tyne and Wear Metro authority and exchanged its allocation to 90 twin-car Metro units. Interestingly the depot did not have any 'steam' connections until 1975 when a surprise visitor was an ex Southern Railway H15 4-6-0, in the area for the S&D 150 Cavalcade, arrived for wheel attention. The only other locomotives known to have been inside the depot were the old North-Eastern electric's, which were stored from about 1946 until 1951, when they were sent for scrap. *I.Falcus.*